G000139004

TRAVELS IN TUSCANY

Charles Spencer

*Illustrations
by Andrea Rauch*

Mandragora

Some of the drawings
in the present volume have been
used by the artist to illustrate the
activities of public bodies
and cultural institutes.
For permission to republish
these drawings the artist
wishes to thank:

Regione Toscana
APT Firenze
Firenze Expo & Congress
Comune di Firenze
Comune di Livorno
Comune di Siena
Santa Maria della Scala, Siena
Teatro Gioco Vita, Piacenza

La Mandragora s.r.l.
piazza Duomo 9, 50122 Firenze
www.mandragora.it

Edited by Mark Roberts

Printed in Italy
ISBN 88-85957-81-1

This book is printed on TCF
(totally chlorine free) paper.

The life of Charles Spencer offers little scope for imaginative speculation. The youngest of the four children of John Spencer and Margaret Mills, Charles was the only one to follow his father's footsteps. In 1914, the year of the elder Spencer's death, he took control of the flourishing solicitor's business, where he had been a partner since 1903.

When the young Charles took his degree at Oxford in 1894, his future path seemed fairly clearly mapped out for him by family tradition. Before taking articles, however, he set out on a tour of Europe, like many a well-to-do young man before him.

Between the winter of 1895 and the spring of '96 he visited Holland, Germany, Austria and Italy; returning through France he reached London in May. In October he began work in his father's office. He never left London again, and passed a secluded and tranquil life in the capital. In 1912 he married Sarah Connor, by whom he had a daughter, named Margaret after his mother.

He died just before the last war, in August 1938, in London.

The only remarkable event in the life of Charles Spencer was the Grand Tour of 1895.

The experience was recorded in a series of notebooks, which lay forgotten in a drawer for years, until they were collected after the author's death by his daughter Margaret, and were privately printed. The edition sank without trace (Charles Spencer, *Tour in Europe*, London 1939).

This was a pity, because Spencer, who had no pretensions as a writer and merely recorded his impressions of his journeys for his own sake, was a curious and in many respects a modern man, capable of deep understanding of the countries and cultures he visited. Attentive above all to the art and architecture of the past, which were his twin passions, he was also prepared to pay close attention to what today we should call social culture. In this connection his observations on food, on popular festivals, and on everyday life, are of the greatest interest.

Spencer had a keen sense of personal privacy. In his book he never once mentions his travelling companions, nor does he bore the reader with tedious accounts of encounters with the many English people living abroad (in Tuscany, the so-called 'anglo-beceri'), whom he undoubtedly did meet. This is a most unusual and attractive omission for an English travel writer.

But it is in his attitude to art that Spencer appears most original. His sympathies (to restrict ourselves to the Tuscan portion of his *Tour*, which we here publish) are for those artists which only the twentieth century was fully to rediscover: Masaccio, Piero della Francesca, Rosso Fiorentino. His critical judgements, although seldom enlarged upon, appear considerably in advance of his times.

What sort of Tuscany is evoked by Spencer's pages? A Tuscany of city-states and bell-towers, of good red wine, of country traditions. In this Tuscany not a word is said about Leonardo da Vinci, and only the briefest mention is made of Michelangelo; but Piero and Caravaggio are lovingly dwelt upon, and so too are wayside votive tabernacles. It is the singular and everyday Tuscany, as seen by a tranquil English traveller, a lover of art and of fine food, prodigal with adjectives, full of good sense.

Herbert Cornwell

2 MAY

Leaving La Spezia in the early morning, we entered Tuscany at midday, and by the late afternoon we were in Carrara.

On our left we passed the Alps, their peaks powdered with marble, and on our right, in the distance, we glimpsed the sea.

The local population seems to derive its character from this situation: ill-tempered and peevish, at times, like mountain people; sunny and gay, frequently, like Mediterranean people.

The mountains are truly spectacular, the shadows at evening standing out against the blue sky, contrasting with the white of the marble quarries...

4 MAY

This morning we clambered up
to the marble quarry of Colonnata.

It was a cruel, proud spectacle:
men cutting the mountain into thick
slices, white as the ham we had eat-
en for breakfast, and which we had
all found so toothsome.

The wounded mountain gives
rise to emotions that transcend time.
Perhaps it was here they cut the
block of marble used by Michael
Angelo for his sublime David...

7 MAY

What strange and mysterious people lived in the valleys and villages of Luni?

What alien gods came down to visit them? How, and when?

Their ancient statues and *cippi* still litter the fields; the peasants use them, familiarly, to mark boundaries, to build their rough dry-stone walls. There are elongated faces and busts, swollen or deformed, with round wide-open eyes – perhaps men, perhaps gods.

Fixed for ever in the silent holiness of ages…

After the silence of the mountains, Pisa appeared to us like a piece of fine lace spread along the banks of the Arno.

The little chapel of the Spina is a prologue to the grandiose poetry of the Piazza dei Miracoli. The green of the meadow, the Cathedral, the Baptistery, the Tower leaning defiantly to one side.

People like to suppose that the Tower leans because of unforeseen subsistence. But how else could it possibly be? In what other way could it laugh at the passage of centuries, and at the follies of man?

15 MAY

I do not remember who said that the Marina di Pisa has the finest sunsets in the world. Whoever it was, was right.

In the late evening the sun plunges into the sea, leaving behind a triumph of colours ranging from gilded yellow to brilliant orange and vermilion red. The sea, which has just swallowed the molten orb, shifts from emerald green to deepest blue.

In the clouds the colours are threads of cream and sugar. The fishermen of Bocca d'Arno wait for the spectacle to end. Then they take up their nets and slowly return to their houses…

21 May

The Fortress of Leghorn reclines in the harbour surrounded by canals, completely isolated from the *terra firma*.

The Livornesi, reputedly an ill-natured and ironical people, claim that the Medici built it there, detached from the city, not to 'defend the Livornesi', but to 'defend themselves from the Livornesi'.

Around the Fortress the system of canals has created a lagoon area, known here as 'the Venice'.

The women of Leghorn are handsome and proud, with dark skin, large eyes, and loud raucous voices.

This morning near the harbour we ate a fish soup, fiery and full of garlic, one of the best I have ever had. It has a strange name, '*caciucco*', which nobody has been able to explain to me.

Opposite the trattoria stands a magnificent monument to Grand Duke Ferdinando, surrounded by chained slaves.

It seems that in Leghorn the captive blackamoors are loved much more than the triumphant prince.

And in fact no-one remembers Ferdinando, but they all speak proudly of '*i quattro mori*'.

24 May

The Livornesi are 'Tuscans of the rocks', and they distinguish themselves disdainfully from the 'Tuscans of the sand'.

Whoever has seen the breakers smashing against the rocks of Cala-furia, and the trees bent by strong winds, will understand the pride of these harsh men, who snatch a pre-carious living from the sea by their repeated daily labours.

The Livornesi love and fear the sea. They curse it, and cannot live without it.

Before setting out to sea again, the sailors of Leghorn, who have just returned from a long voyage, offer prayers and thanksgiving to the Madonna di Montenero.

Usually those who climb the Monte take with them a votive painting to leave at the shrine.

These pictures show wonderful scenes of storms at sea, ships struck by lightning, extraordinary and perilous encounters, and how the Virgin intercedes on behalf of her faithful clients.

The walls of Montenero tell of a story of simple and devout fisher-folk, a story of absence and longing.

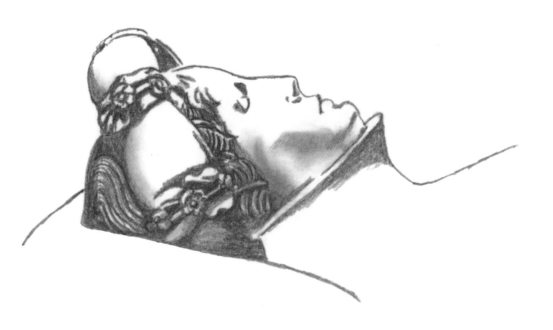

29 May

Lucca. The young Ilaria sleeps with her hands crossed on her breast. The corners of her mouth turn upwards in a sly and mischievous smile.

The little dog at her feet is waiting for her to wake up and throw a stick or a stone for him to retrieve.

There is nothing in this monument which Jacopo has left in the cathedral of San Martino to remind us of death...

Ilaria recalls the maidens in certain Nordic legends. She is the Sleeping Beauty, awaiting the kiss that will rouse her. Waiting thus, her stony sleep is calm and serene.

We went up to Borgo di Mozzano, and found the Devil.

You should know (for so the locals told us) that once upon a time Saint Julian the Hospitaller needed to build a bridge, and sought assistance from the Evil One. He, of course, demanded in exchange the first soul to cross the completed bridge.

Saint Julian promised, and the Devil built the bridge in a single night's work. In the morning, while the people looked on in amazement, Old Nick demanded his reward. But Saint Julian chased a dog over the bridge, and thus swindled the Devil.

So enraged was he that with one kick of his cloven hoof he caused the bridge to assume the curious shape we see today.

3 JUNE

Reaching Pistoia in the late evening, we found decent lodging at the Locanda del Leone Bianco.

Early in the morning, skirting the Piazza del Duomo, we strolled as far as the old Hospital of the Ceppo. Here there is a frieze of polychrome terracotta, made by the workshop of Giovanni Della Robbia, showing the seven Corporal Works of Mercy.

Separating the scenes are some delightful allegories (such as Prudence, shown as a the head of a young girl gazing into a look-glass, with the face of an old man on the back of her head). Brilliantly coloured harpies mount guard at the corners of the building…

4 JUNE

The administrative territory of the city of Pistoia is very large and stretches as far as the mountains which separate Tuscany from Emilia. So it is not surprising that the city's symbol should be a mountain bear (here known by the curious name of 'micco'), wrapped in a checked mantle.

We found him all over the city, from the Palazzo Pubblico to the Palace of the Knights of the Tau.

The mantle is checky gules and argent and according to the learned derives from the battle-standard of the mediaeval Comune. But the people say it represents the colours of Saint James, patron of Pistoia.

6 JUNE

Prato. On a rainy day in late
spring the sudden apparition of
the cathedral pulpit, with its stu-
pendous '*cantoria*' by Donatello,
seemed to everyone like a ray of
sunshine piercing the clouds. The
marble children dance and sing,
touching hands lightly, following
one another in an endless musical
round.

One could spend hours gazing
at them, watching the interplay of
shadow, changing the point of
view, renewing the miracle at every
moment.

After three days of tedious and depressing drizzle (which complicated our journey in no small measure), Florence appeared in pale sunshine, and with a rainbow right above the dome of Santa Maria del Fiore.

The sight of Bunelleschi's dome together with the rainbow seemed a good omen for our sojourn, from which I expect great things.

We have taken rooms at the hotel on the Via Porta Rossa, very near the Duomo, and a short walk from the square which the Florentines still insist on calling 'the Piazza of the Grand Duke'.

From tomorrow we begin to breathe the air of the Renaissance. This evening we retired to bed warmed by the good red wine they produce in the surrounding hills…

For some days, as though suffering indigestion from so much beauty, I have been unable to record the marvels that crowd into the eyes and heart.

Even a brief visit to the Uffizi would suffice to fill an entire book with notes, sketches and observations. In a single room there are more wonderful things than one could decently hope to see in an entire lifetime.

An angel musician, marvellously painted by Rosso, chimes with the Cupid shooting his fiery dart in Botticelli's Primavera...

This is but one of the endless correspondences one lights upon strolling from room to room...

24 JUNE

In a passage inside Palazzo Vecchio a Flemish painter, who worked
with Vasari on the structure of the
building, has painted a scene showing an exuberant display of fireworks in the Piazza of the Grand
Duke. This evening too the streets
will be lit up with fireworks in honour of Saint John the Baptist, patron of Florence.

There is a girlish sense of expec-
tation in the city. As soon as supper
is ended the people will pour out of
their houses and line the banks of
the river, waiting to see the '*fochi*'.

There are stalls set up, selling
sweets and spinning toys known as
'*girandole*'.

Before returning to the hotel to
dine, we have become accustomed
to take a short walk along the Lun-
garni. We generally take the right
bank and without hurrying go as
far as the Ponte alla Carraia, or
sometimes a little further.

Walking back towards the Porta Rossa we enjoy the magnificent
view of the Ponte Vecchio, against
the green hills in the distance.

The Arno, just before the moon
rises, glimmers with a silvery light.
Its clear waters glide towards the
sea unimpeded by the sand-banks
and grassy mud-flats. Such final
and perfect beauty as nothing could
ever alter…

28 JUNE

The Florentines, an obstinate and contrary people, have no love for tyrants or for the powerful. And the Piazza del Granduca, the city's show-case, is filled with symbols of this inclination of theirs.

Here Michael Angelo's David makes ready his sling, Perseus holds up the severed head of Medusa, Hercules crushes the giant Cacus, Judith raises her sword to strike at the neck of Holofernes.

For 'Fiorenza', the City of the Flower, what symbol could be more suitable that the fleur-de-lis?

"*Per division fatto vermiglio*" says Dante, recalling the bloody strife between Guelfs and Ghibellines. All over Florence the stones bear emblems and devices.

In a chapel in Santa Maria Novella we found a rather unusual one, a wobbly duckling, on the arms of the Ubriachi, or 'Drunkards', family: *nomina sunt consequentia rerum*?

30 JUNE

In the chapel of Palazzo Medici
on Via Larga, Benozzo Gozzoli has
frescoed the young Lorenzo as one
of the Three Kings, at the head of a
magnificent procession wending
its way to pay homage to the Christ
Child.

The procession passes through a
landscape where the Biblical scene
mingles with the familiar Florentine hills.

Perhaps Lorenzo discussed such
a scene and such a landscape with
his philosopher and artist friends in
the Orto di San Marco. It is a landscape of myth and allegory, offering
glimpses of Utopia.

2 JULY

The real miracle of the Florentine Renaissance is the architecture: the buildings of Leon Battista Alberti and of Filippo Brunelleschi.

The new humanist vision expressed in such architecture draws upon the world of antiquity: Man is placed at the centre of creation, both artistic and divine.

It is a sunny, bold and serene architecture, that of Santa Maria Novella and the Duomo, of Santo Spirito and the Palazzo Rucellai.

Man, in the work of Filippo Brunelleschi, is able to look straight into the face of his Creator...

4 JULY

We arrived at Pratolino in the late morning, and after a light collation of cheese and salad we visited the Medici villa. As we rounded the drive we came upon the colossal statue of Appennino, sculpted by Giambologna.

It is a strange and impressive sight. The giant seems to be tired, crouching on one knee, his head bowed, as though exhausted by the rigours of the winter. Behind him a dragon with gaping jaws flaps its wings, but seems too heavy to fly.

The park is beautifully kept. It stretches down the valley almost as far as the first houses of Florence.

Of the paintings we saw in Palazzo Pitti the ones that remain in my mind are the canvases of Raphael.

How different they are from the titanic masculinity of Michael Angelo! With Raphael, everything seems dissolved in sweetness and languor. The Madonnas have the same composed beauty sometimes encountered in the women of Florence, while the babies are pink and chubby. The setting is always an idyllic landscape.

A goldfinch flies down to play with Saint John and the Christ Child.

Michelangelo da Caravaggio is as unquiet and tormented as Raphael is serene. What painterly power there is, behind those coarse and plebeian faces!

The Bacchus we admired in the Uffizi is undoubtedly a baker's lad, dressed up by chance or for fun in a sheet and some vine-leaves. He is still a fresh and blooming youth, but his sad eyes presage a harsh life as an adult.

We saw this same tormented, proletarian art in the Saint Matthew in Berlin. There the feet and knee of the seated Evangelist are thrust rudely into the foreground, augmenting the power of the composition and its provocative charge.

8 July

Masaccio occupies a special place in our hearts. He represents the triumph of Man, and the regeneration of painting after the chilly refinement of fourteenth-century Gothic art. Masaccio came to Florence from the countryside of the Arno valley, and died young. Yet in a short time, and with comparatively few works, he unleashed a revolution without precedent. His Madonnas still have the sacred majesty of the fourteenth century, but now the Child sucks his fingers, or smiles at his mother.

Such tiny gestures alter the entire conception of art. After Masaccio painting could never be the same again.

To reach Arezzo we decided to follow the road through the Casentino. It is perhaps but the easiest but certainly the most fascinating, with ruins of former greatness in strange contrast with a harsh and isolated present.

Towards evening we arrived at Ponte di Poppi, and found lodgings with a family living on the edge of the town.

Local legend has it that on the level open plain one can still hear the clash of arms from the battle of Campaldino. The old people will swear that they have heard these noises. People speak of experiencing strange and disturbing visions while crossing the plain at night.

Today being Sunday our hosts prepared for us '*ravioli*' with herbs and ricotta cheese, and invited us to do them justice. They were really delicious.

The most memorable moment occurred after luncheon, in the middle of the afternoon, when the old grandmother gathered the little ones around her (four or five of them, I suppose), and began to tell them stories which made their hair stand on end. She spoke rapidly in Tuscan dialect and we understood almost nothing. I was very sorry about this because, as we afterwards gathered, she was telling the old tales of the valley, about witches and the Devil, scheming friars and enchanted maidens.

I should very much have liked to learn something of the magical Casentino and its wonders.

13 JULY

Arezzo: in the apse of the church of San Francesco the city is reflected as in a mirror. The houses in the backgrounds of Piero's wonderful frescoes confront us as soon as we turn the corner of the street, with the very same pointed roofs and steep lanes.

Even the people of Arezzo seem to have stepped out of Piero's frescoes. Both men and women have broad faces and high cheek-bones, strong necks and pink cheeks.

14 July

Piero's landscape can be studied in the frescoes of the *Legend of the True Cross*.

The Tiber runs slowly and the houses are reflected in its waters. Piero dei Franceschi tells stories from this isolated corner of Tuscany, so close to the borders of Umbria and the Marches: Duke Federigo, blind in one eye, hacked at his own nose with his sword, the better to see his enemy in battle; his beloved wife Battista, who died young, is pale and distant.

To reach the Chianti and the Val d'Elsa we crossed the entire Val d'Ambra today, from Levane to the Colonna del Grillo.

The valley of the Ambra is carefully cultivated, and most beautiful. The towns are mostly small, and perched on hilly peaks.

The most extraordinary sight was a cypress near the Colonna, the tallest I have ever seen. It is perhaps a hundred feet high, and takes three men to embrace its trunk. At the top it is divided into two. It marks a bend in the road, and can be seen from miles away.

Approaching the Chianti, we put up for the night near the castle of Volpaia. A strong red wine warmed the whole company.

18 JULY

Monteriggioni marks the end of the Chianti and the beginning of the Val d'Elsa. We saw it from a distance, crowned with towers, as Dante describes it. Inside the walls time seems to have stood still, in a glorious and distant past, as at San Gimignano ('of the beautiful towers', as the saying goes), which boasts its centuries of history with proud defiance.

Mediaeval Tuscany had a predilection for slim tall buildings, each striving to overtop the others and reach the heavens... whether to converse with the Almighty, to scrutinise the horizon for approaching enemies, would be hard to say.

20 July

Leaving Colle Val d'Elsa on the road for Volterra we turned off to the left to admire the solitary little church of Conèo.

It is extraordinary how much Tuscan architecture makes use of decoration in polychrome marbles. We saw in Florence and Pistoia the harmonious alternating of white, black and green marble.

At Conèo the stone is interspersed by regular rows of red brick. In the raking evening light the façade flames with gold.

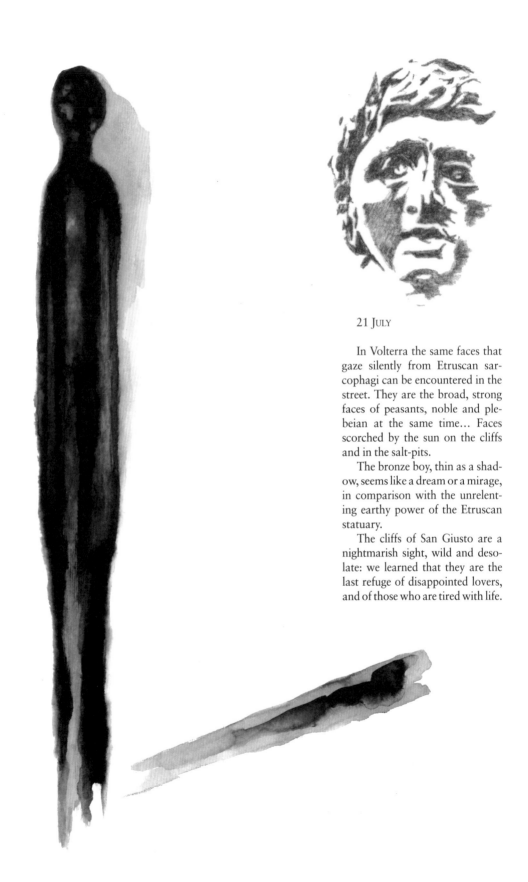

21 July

In Volterra the same faces that gaze silently from Etruscan sarcophagi can be encountered in the street. They are the broad, strong faces of peasants, noble and plebeian at the same time... Faces scorched by the sun on the cliffs and in the salt-pits.

The bronze boy, thin as a shadow, seems like a dream or a mirage, in comparison with the unrelenting earthy power of the Etruscan statuary.

The cliffs of San Giusto are a nightmarish sight, wild and desolate: we learned that they are the last refuge of disappointed lovers, and of those who are tired with life.

23 JULY

On the road for Sienna we turned south to visit the monastery of San Galgano, its stones and bricks abandoned for centuries. The roof has fallen in, and the church is open to the sky; where the pavement was, lush grass now grows.

In the nearby chapel of Montesiepi we found King Arthur.

Or rather, we found a sword thrust into a rock, awaiting the coming of a king. But unlike Arthur, the Blessed Galgano Guidotti abandoned his sword on purpose, to stand here like a cross, when he renounced the military life.

We saw the story of Galgano and his sword on the walls of the chapel, wonderfully frescoed by Ambrogio Lorenzetti.

24 July

Back on the road to Sienna, just before the village of Rosia we came upon a hump-backed bridge, built of stone, known as the 'Ponte della Pia'.

Legend has it that Pia dei Tolomei passed over it on her way to death in the Maremma at the hands of her jealous husband Nello della Pietra. It is a story to rival that of Othello and Desdemona.

The wicked Ghino di Tacco made advances to the virtuous Pia and was of course repulsed, so he accused her of adultery. Blinded by jealousy, her husband had her put to death.

Too late did Nello discover the constancy of his wife, in time only to mourn her.

Pia dei Tolomei still lives in the Siennese memory. Tragedies are written and songs sung about her.

Dante puts into her mouth the famous words: "*Siena mi fe', disfecemi Maremma…*"

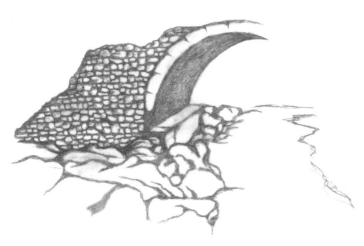

Like Monteriggioni and San Gimignano, Sienna appeared in the distance with the irregular outline of its towers and spires.

As at Florence, after an afternoon of light rain a pale rainbow arose over the city. Once again, a good omen.

Our expectations in Sienna are similar to those we had in Florence. Although completely different, both cities are unspoilt and filled with art and tradition.

We have found lodgings in the Pian dei Mantellini, near the Duomo and not far from the Campo.

26 JULY

A short walk took us up the hill past the church of San Domenico. From the top the view of the Duomo is breath-taking. The cathedral of Santa Maria Assunta is striped with black and white marble, and spreads itself over the acropolis of Sienna, dominating the roofs of the houses and raising its tall *campanile* towards God.

To think that this great Christian edifice was to have been, in the dreams of fourteenth-century Sienna, immeasurably greater, and that the present nave was to have been merely a transept... The arrival of the Black Death put an end to the dream, and brought the Siennese back to earth.

The Campo is certainly one of the biggest town squares I have ever seen, and it is one of the most unusual, its shell-like form being divided into regular segments.

I will say nothing of the magnificence of the tower, and its almost incredible height, nor of the elegance of the Palazzo, like a stage-set in a theatre, expecting applause.

I was struck by tiny details. The water-spouts at the extremities of the entablature on the 'cappella di piazza', for example, are carved into winged monsters, half men and half beasts, goats and dragons.

There is a fantastical quality to the Siennese imagination which until now I had associated only with Northern Europe.

SECVRI: TAS.

29 July

Inside the Palazzo, Ambrogio Lorenzetti painted his ideal city, with its safe streets, its citizens practising peaceable and lucrative commerce, and its pretty girls holding hands as they dance.

Seated above are the allegories of the virtues essential for good government. Peace and Justice preside over the general prosperity. Bad Government, with its demon's face and pointed teeth, might cast a blight over everything.

Ambrogio's city is no different from the one we have been visiting in these days. Brick, white and black marble, narrow twisting streets, steep ascents, arches, noble palaces...

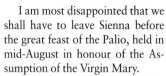

I am most disappointed that we shall have to leave Sienna before the great feast of the Palio, held in mid-August in honour of the Assumption of the Virgin Mary.

The Palio is a horse race, which everyone says is most dangerous and difficult, run around the Piazza del Campo. Twice a year ten of the city's eighteen wards take part in the race.

The people here seem to talk of little else, and their enthusiasm is contagious.

This city loves its Palio and especially the horse, which as the principal participant is caressed and cosseted. Before the race it is led into church and blessed by the priest.

Continual talk about the Palio, the songs we hear all over town, the beating of drums and twirling of flags (even the children are getting ready for the procession) have turned our attention to the horse. We find him everywhere, in marble in the Duomo, and in frescoes in the Palazzo.

We were reminded of others we have seen, such as the marvellous one ridden by Sir John Hawkwood in the Cathedral of Florence...

Tuscany is a land dominated by '*campanilismo*', the fierce spirit of local allegiance. Speak of Pisa in Leghorn and see what happens to you! Or of Sienna in Florence. These are centuries-old rivalries; the results of bloody wars, without quarter given or expected.

We travelled south and after a few miles were at Montaperti.

This was the scene of that memorable battle which '*fece l'Arbia colorata in rosso*', when the Florentine troops were routed.

It took place in 1260 but nobody seems to know for sure where. The Siennese point to a hillock crowned with cypresses, which according to them was the eye of the cyclone.

Here the Siennese cat met the Florentine dog. From here they both retired to lick their wounds, and prepare for the next and bloodiest encounter.

On the road for Montalcino we traversed a bare and apparently desolate region known as the Crete. And the hills really are of '*creta*' or clay, scorched by the August sun and drought. The soil is almost black but seems fertile, for the sods have just been turned for a new sowing in the autumn. I can picture the succession of the seasons here: the green corn sprouting in the spring, ripening into gold in summer, lying hidden throughout the winter.

The sinuous outline of the Crete, the colours, the rise and fall of seasons, make one think of a woman's body: now young and unripe, now florid and Buxton, now – alas! – wrinkly and undesirable.

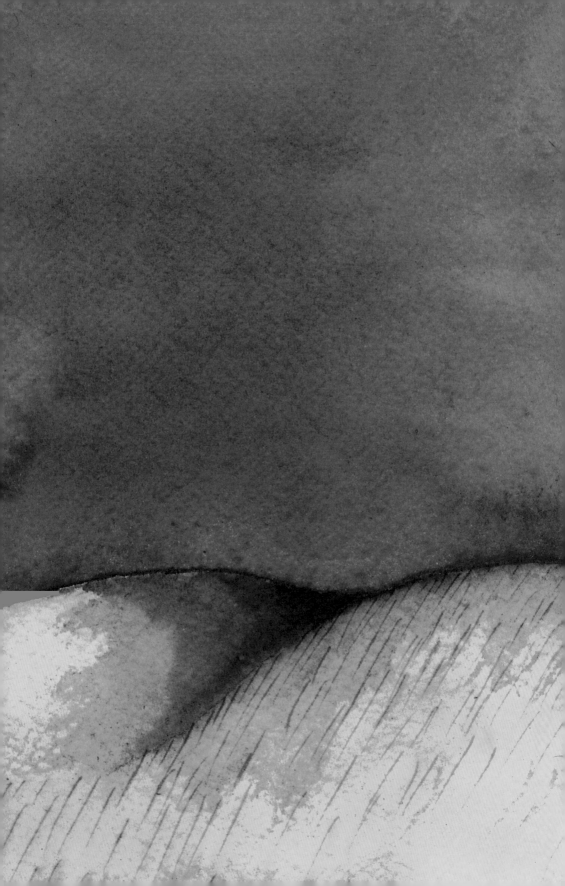

5 August

The south of Tuscany is singularly rich in large solitary churches, hermitages and monasteries, magnificent both in architecture and in conception.

There are active monastic communities, such as Monteoliveto, and isolated churches like San Biagio outside Montepulciano.

It seems that Christian piety sought to withdraw itself from the temptations of the city, but was unwilling to renounce the magnificence within which man has always striven to conduct a dialogue with God.

7 August

The Abbey of Sant'Antimo is also isolated, enclosed within a ver-
dant valley and surrounded by ancient olive-groves.

We arrived in the late afternoon.
The sinking sun lent a pinkish glow
to the façade of the Abbey. The
evening air was warm, and the pink
marble flamed with gold.

A great and touching spectacle.
Perfect peace.

Supper, a somewhat modest one
to tell the truth, was accompanied
by an excellent red wine from Montalcino.

9 AUGUST

Here there are great churches, strong and magnificent hermitages, but also little buildings and modest way-side tabernacles, put there for popular devotion. They are often found at a cross-roads, marking the way and calling for a moment's prayer or recollection. The images they contain are of humble materials, but are redolent of history.

The 'Madonna of the Seven Sorrows' has her breast pierced with swords, in pity for the sufferings of Christ; the 'Madonna of Comfort' was chosen as an emblem during the reactionary uprisings of '99, the result of fanatical intolerance in Sienna and Arezzo.

But the Virgin was innocent of the barbarities committed in her name…

The final image of our Tuscan journey that remains in our memory is the white castle of Talamone, overlooking the sea.

Perhaps it was also the first image we saw, three months ago, as we entered Tuscany from the Apuan Alps. A white quarry, the marble sliced in great cubes from the belly of the mountain.

Those very slices of marble seem to have been transported here to build the castle, so as to create a constant image of the Tuscany we are now on the point of leaving.

For it is time to direct our steps towards Rome...

Travels in Tuscany

Printed by Alpilito - Florence
May 2000